Teen
magazine

The Rules

FOR TEENS

Meg Schneider

W9-BWW-284

SCHOLASTIC INC.
New York Toronto London Auckland Sydney
Mexico City New Delhi Hong Kong

No part of this publication may be reproduced in whole or in part, or stored in a retrieval system or transmitted in any form by any means, electronic, mechanical, photocopying, recording, or otherwise, without written permission of the publisher. For information regarding permission, write to Scholastic Inc., Attention: Permissions Dept., 555 Broadway, New York, NY 10012.

ISBN 0-439-11464-0

Distributed under license from
The Petersen Publishing Company, L.L.C.
Copyright © 2000 The Petersen Publishing
Company, L.L.C. All rights reserved.
Published by Scholastic Inc.

 Produced by 17th Street Productions,
an Alloy Online, Inc. company
33 West 17th Street
New York, NY 10011

Teen Teen is a trademark of Petersen
Publishing Company, L.L.C.

SCHOLASTIC and associated logos are trademarks and/or
registered trademarks of Scholastic Inc.

12 11 10 9 8 7 6 5 4 3 2   0/0 1 2 3 4 5

Printed in the U.S.A.   01
First Scholastic printing, August 2000

TABLE OF CONTENTS

INTRODUCTION

Someone is always asking you to follow their rules. In school, in sports, at home—rules are everywhere. Your teachers may have certain rules about the way your homework must look when you turn it in. Your parents may have certain rules about how late you can stay out on a weekend night. Your coach may have rules for how to behave at away games. You name it—there are rules for everything. So why would you want to follow more rules when you're going on a first date or flirting with the hottie in your English class? Well, it's simple. Rules are meant to help you out. They offer something solid that you can always count on. Rules are cool!

The thing about the word *rule* is that it sounds so absolute, like there are no other options. *The Rules for Teens* offers advice, not laws. Whether you decide to make the first move on your crush or tell your boyfriend you need to make time for your girlfriends is ultimately up to you. You may find you need to bend the rules a little or adjust them to fit your particular situation. But remember, they're here for you when you need a voice of reason or a little guidance.

Relationships are never easy, and sometimes

it's hard to know just what to do and say. *The Rules for Teens* will help you feel confident and strong about every move you make. So read on and remember: It's cool to follow the rules!

IF YOU WANT
TO ASK A GUY
OUT, GO FOR
IT! YOU CAN
SURVIVE A NO.

YOU'RE STANDING AT THE BUS stop, talking to Josh. You're dying to ask him to go to Sarah's party with you. But you've never asked a guy out before. You'd feel so much better if he'd just ask you instead.

Only it doesn't seem like he's going to ask you or anyone else, for that matter. Maybe he's not into parties. Or maybe he's one of those guys who doesn't like going to parties with a date. Maybe he doesn't like you! You won't be able to really tell unless you ask. . . .

BUT WHAT IF HE SAYS NO?!

So in other words, only *he* should take that risk?

That's so unfair!

Every time a boy asks a girl out, he's risking a

rejection. Why shouldn't a girl have to take that chance, also?

Yes, back in the Stone Age, girls would have been considered superaggressive and pushy if they dared to ask a boy out. But let's face it—things have changed!

Today girls who ask boys out are usually considered pretty cool. They tend to be self-confident, easygoing, and even considerate. After all, doing the asking takes the pressure off the boy! Also, think of how you feel when a boy asks you out. It's flattering, right? Boys feel the same way when the situation is reversed.

Of course, once you decide to take the "asking" plunge, you're faced with a whole new problem.

What if the answer is no? What will you say? Do? Think?

Remember, a lot of what you will say, do, think, or feel will depend on the form of the rejection. Obviously an "I can't. I'm not going to the party. I have plans with my family," is a no you can take. "I can't. I've already made plans with a bunch of guys from the swim team," is another no you can probably handle. But answers like, "I can't. I'm going with Mikayla," or, "I think I'd rather go on my own," might be tougher to take.

"I asked this guy I really liked to go to the movies. He'd been so friendly toward me, I thought it was no big deal. But then he said he couldn't because he was busy with other friends, which I was sure wasn't true, and he looked really uncomfortable. So I made up some lame excuse and took off. I felt pretty bummed . . . but I still think it was cool I got it together to ask.**"** —Jessie

You might feel foolish for thinking he would say yes, hurt that he doesn't seem interested in you, and angry that you put yourself on the line. Those are all understandable feelings, and you have a right to them. Maybe you'll cry alone or go to a friend's house and confess you just did the dumbest, most embarrassing thing. You might even spend a sleepless night, worrying that everyone in the world will think you're a jerk if they find out. But guess what? You should feel proud, not embarrassed. You aren't afraid to get out there and ask for what you want. You're not stuck living in the Stone Age! Good for you!

And what if he says no? Probably the best way to go is to keep calm and say something simple like, "Okay. I just thought I'd ask," before walking away. You shouldn't feel the need to put yourself through further possibly awkward conversation, especially in the mood you're now in!

And don't be surprised if in the near future he asks *you* out.

Huh?

It's simple. He may not have asked you out because it didn't occur to him that you were interested. Now that he knows you definitely are, next time *he* might be the one to make the first move.

JUST BECAUSE A
GUY IS HOT
DOESN'T MEAN
HE'S FOR YOU.

JAMES IS SO HOT. HE'S GOT A great body, sexy dark eyes, and a perfect smile. He's the captain of the basketball team, too. The thing is, you're kind of a brain, and he's not. (He's really not.) In fact, he doesn't read much or talk about too many things besides sports.

Still, he's a great kisser. And your friends can't believe you're going out with him. The only problem is, you're bored to death when you're with him.

WHAT SHOULD YOU DO?

It's amazing how getting a popular guy can feel like a major accomplishment. It's sort of like winning the first-place trophy at your next track meet.

Only in this case, the trophy is walking and talking!

The thing is, you know he's not *really* a trophy. No one is. He just looks good—especially next to you.

Not that you shouldn't enjoy getting special attention from a superpopular guy. But do you like other things about him besides his looks?

If you have nothing in common and you're bored when you're with him, you're definitely not going to have much fun together. And then you're going to have to deal with breaking up with him, and breakups aren't fun. In fact, breakups can involve all kinds of unnecessary insecurities and pain—especially when the relationship was never actually *real*.

Admittedly, going out with the cutest boy in your school can be a big ego boost—if he chose you, then you must be pretty hot yourself. But then again, if you're so hot, what do you need him for? You don't!

And what if he breaks up with you? You might wind up thinking, I'm such a loser. How could I have ever believed that a good-looking guy like that would stay interested in me? You won't be hurting over love lost. You'll be suffering from a bad case of low self-esteem, and that's a lot harder to shake off than a boy you don't really like.

And once you've realized your mistake and you decide to break up with him . . .

News flash! Great-looking boys have feelings, too!

It isn't fair to pretend to care for someone who you feel, deep down inside, hardly connects with you at all. You might even wind up breaking his heart, and *then* how will you feel?

"I guess you could say I'm a pretty popular guy. I'm decent looking. Girls like me. But one girl I went out with I could tell wasn't all that into me. She just wanted to drag me places. I felt like she wanted to show me off or something. I tried to talk to her, but she was just into herself. When I broke up with her, she was pretty pissed off, but I didn't care." —David

So what do you do?

No matter how cute he is, don't get into a boyfriend-girlfriend thing until you have true feelings . . . not just a surface attraction. How can you tell the difference?

Well, when he's talking, do you wish he'd be quiet so you can just kiss? Would you rather go out with him and loads of other people than be alone together? Do you find yourself really enjoying the first few minutes of the date when you first see him and then about a half hour later feeling kind of lonely or bored or both?

If the answer to any of these questions is yes, then you can pretty much bet there's not a lot happening between the two of you. You'd probably be better off doing the *friend* thing and leaving the *boyfriend* thing for someone you're really into in *all* ways, not just looks.

Having a hot date can be fun, even if you don't find him all that fascinating. But having a hot *boyfriend* you don't like that much will inevitably end on a sour note.

And the funny thing is, after a while he'll stop looking so hot.

DON'T SPILL
YOUR GUTS
ON A FIRST
DATE.

YOU'RE OUT FOR THE FIRST TIME with Michael, and the two of you are talking as he walks you home from your date. He's just finished telling you a cute story about his dad, and now he wants to know what your parents are like.

You don't know what to say.

Part of you wants to blurt out, "They have a terrible marriage, they're constantly harassing me about my grades, my sister can do no wrong, and I can't wait to leave the house in the morning," but you stop yourself.

It seems too heavy and way too depressing.

But you're not sure why he should mind. After all, it's not his life.

It's not that it's not his life. It's that it's too early for him to take on *yours*. Definitely at a certain point in a relationship, we all want to tell those close to us how we really feel about things. But it's always a good idea to start out just enjoying each other's company and holding back some of the more intense thoughts and feelings.

This is because another person's pain can be sort of scary. Two people on a first date haven't had enough fun, easy, cool times together to balance out the "bad" news. If you start yakking his ear off with stories about your difficulties at home before he gets to know you, he might think, Oh, wow, this girl has got more problems than I can handle.

But if you wait awhile until you've had some fun together, he's more likely to think, She's so great to be with. I never knew she had so many problems at home. Maybe I can make her laugh today.

"I was out with this new girl, Yvette, and we started talking about her parents and how they don't understand who she is and she started to cry. I felt sorry for her, but the truth is

I kind of wished she'd lighten up. I wanted to have some fun. See if I even liked her and all. I felt kind of selfish, but I couldn't help it. I mean, my friend has similar problems, and I don't mind listening, but on a first date it's sort of hard to handle." —Angel

It's not that boys are insensitive, or that they only like girls who act happy all the time, or that they don't want to listen or help—not at all. It's just that it's always hard to know just what to say to people who are wrestling with big problems, especially if you don't know them all that well. Maybe your problems remind them of their own, which makes them uncomfortable. Maybe they've never experienced that kind of pain, and so what's being said feels foreign to them. Whatever it is, the two of you will be able to help each other through difficult times far better after you've gotten to know each other.

Of course, if he asks you a specific question, you don't need to lie, either. "Oh, everything is great. My parents are the best. We're the happiest family on the planet!" is hardly necessary. If you say simply, "Well, I have some problems with my parents, but I'm managing," that's fine. Your first date doesn't have to sound like an episode of *Oprah*.

So if you love to laugh, let him hear that. If you love to dance, let him see that. If you love to talk about the future, let him hear that. And then, when you feel a special closeness building between the two of you and something is bothering you, you can begin to share the bad stuff with him, too.

By then it won't feel foreign to him. He'll be comfortable enough with you to see that your thoughts and feelings are just another part of the special and lovable you.

ENJOY THE
DATE. DON'T
KEEP TAKING
ITS
TEMPERATURE.

SO FAR, SO GOOD, CLAIRE SAID TO herself as she and Rob walked into the party. We seem to be hitting it off pretty well. Then Rob headed off into the living room.

Uh-oh, she thought. Rob hadn't taken her hand, put his arm around her, or anything. And now he was off in the corner, laughing with his friend Kevin. What did that mean? Maybe he was glad to get away from her.

Claire searched the room. Thank God. There was her friend Sara. She had started to edge toward Sara, feeling just a little upset, when Rob returned to her side.

"Miss me?" he joked, grabbing her hand and smiling.

Okay, maybe I'm overreacting, Claire decided. I mean, everything seems to be okay now. Right?

Imagine if you had a fever and desperately wanted it to go away so that tomorrow night you could go to an important dance. Every five minutes you take your temperature. First it's 102, and you're upset. Then ten minutes later it's 101, and you feel better. But fifteen minutes later it's 102.5. You just want to die. You'll drive yourself crazy, and in the end what really matters is that you're sick, you need rest, and if you get some sleep, your fever might actually be gone in the morning.

It's kind of the same thing with a date. You might have a really funny moment, then you might suddenly feel a bit awkward with each other. Then, all of a sudden, you might share something about yourselves that brings you closer. These ups and downs are perfectly normal. If you get overexcited every time there's an up moment, only to come crashing down when there's a little awkwardness between you, you won't enjoy the date.

What you need to do is stop taking the date's temperature.

Just sit back, let the date play out, and see what happens. If it feels good, great, if it feels tense, you can try to warm things up, but in either case don't draw conclusions. Don't think, Oh, this is *so* perfect! or, Oh no! Everything is going downhill! because if you start reacting to every little thing that happens on your date, you'll end up getting totally stressed out. You'll feel desperate to keep the good feelings flowing or to stop the bad feelings from contaminating everything. You'll be working so hard at maintaining things or fixing things that you won't respond naturally or spontaneously to anything. And you won't be very much fun.

"I thought I was going to lose my mind. We were talking in front of my locker, and he laughed real loud at something I said and I felt great . . . like he really liked me. Then I made another comment, and he shrugged and said, "I don't really care about that kind of stuff." I was worrying that he thought maybe we had nothing in common. Later he put his hand on my back and I thought, Cool, he's into me. Then he dropped it and I thought, Now what did I do?!" —Kim

If you stop worrying and relax, a natural ebb and flow will take over. And that natural ebb and flow will represent the way the two of you honestly relate. When you work at a date, you're not being yourself. When you're simply on it, allowing things to take their course, you are.

So leave the thermometer home. When it's all over, you can consider how the date went overall. But even then try not to pull it apart into little pieces, worrying about this or that moment. Think of it as a whole. And have a little confidence.

People are usually left with the same general impression. If you think the date went well, chances are so did he.

DON'T
EXPECT HIM
TO PAY FOR
EVERYTHING.

IT'S HAPPENING. TIM ASKED YOU out to the movies, and now you're in line at the ticket window. This is so cool, you think. Tim seems to really like you. You even held hands as soon as you got out of his parents' car.

You're thinking about how great it feels to be "taken out" when suddenly you hear Tim say, "Gillian, your ticket is seven-fifty."

WHAT?? Did he just ask you for money? You try to hide your disappointment, but it's hard. You were thinking this date was like a grown-up thing. . . .

For some girls (not all!) there's something very romantic about being "taken out." This is largely because it's the first cousin to being "taken care of," and that can be a very comforting feeling. But it certainly isn't a feeling you *need* in order to experience real romance.

Besides, the notion that the man is responsible for paying for everything went out of style a long time ago.

Yes, it's true that many men who have jobs often pay for the woman's share of the date when they take them out. But not *always*. Why should they? Chances are the woman works, too, and may even earn more money than her date. It isn't fair for the woman to expect him to pay every single time. These days it's common for men and women to share date expenses fifty-fifty unless they're celebrating a special occasion like a birthday or anniversary, in which case one person might want to treat the other and pay for the whole date.

Like you, the guy you're going out with may have a part-time job or earn pocket money by baby-sitting, or maybe his parents give him an allowance. And he's probably using that money to save for things like a new pair of skates, a CD, a computer game, or even college.

And he may really *want* to cough up the cash for your dinner or movie ticket or ride on the roller coaster or whatever, but there's a good chance he just doesn't have it. There's also a good chance that he knows you expect him to pay, but he still can't. Don't hold that against him.

The fact that he *can't* shouldn't stand in the way of your feelings for him. He obviously likes you a lot. He's asked you out. He wants to be with you alone, to share a meal or a movie and maybe hold your hand. But he's not an adult. He's a teenager—he's still in school and can't have a full-time job—and therefore his cash flow is probably limited.

"I could tell Brooke was upset that I didn't pay for her admission to our school carnival. I could tell because she hadn't even reached for her bag until she saw I didn't pay for her, and then she got real quiet. I felt bad, but I mean, where was I supposed to get the money to pay for two tickets?"

—Marc

Of course, you might find yourself out with a boy who does pay for you. It could be because he spends his money mainly on his social life. Or maybe his parents gave him some money to spend on the date. That's nice. But that's really all it is. It's actually a nonevent when it comes to romance. Your date is caring for you more when he puts his arm around you when you're shivering in the stands watching a football game on a cold day than he is when paying for your movie ticket.

One last note. There are lots of girls who wouldn't hear of letting someone pay their way on a date. In fact, they might be resentful if their date even offered. They might think, Wait a minute. Don't patronize me! I can pay for myself. I can take care of myself. It's doubtful that a guy who offers to pay is actually trying to put you down. He wants your date to go well just as badly as you do.

But the fact is, money isn't an indication of caring. If he has it, great. If he doesn't, that's fine, too. No one can buy love or romance. Don't be disappointed if you have to reach for your wallet or purse. It may be the only way the two of you can go to the movies together!

DON'T GO IN THE
CORNER TO
GIGGLE WITH
YOUR GIRLFRIEND
WHEN YOU'RE OUT
WITH A GUY.

YOU'RE AT MCDONALD'S WITH ZACH and a bunch of friends. You and Zach have been getting kind of close lately. The two of you are sitting in the corner of a big booth with your friends when Abby suddenly turns to you and says, "Oh, Jen, remember what happened last Saturday night!" referring to the weird guy who tried to pick the two of you up at the skating rink. You start laughing. "That was so funny. . . ."

Zach looks at you quizzically. "What happened?"

"Oh, nothing." You giggle, rolling your eyes at Abby and blushing. You don't want Zach to know about it, anyway. He'd be hurt.

Zach slowly pulls his arm from around your shoulders and smiles weakly at his friend sitting across from him.

YOU'RE NOT SURE WHAT'S WRONG.

What's wrong is something you probably learned when you were young and your mom told you, "Don't whisper in front of other people! It makes them feel left out!" This is just a more grown-up version of the same thing. It isn't nice to joke or talk secretively about things others can't share. It's rude, plain and simple. How would you like it if you were asked to hang out with a group of kids and then a bunch of them started a conversation in a foreign language you couldn't understand? You'd wonder why you were there. You'd wonder what they were saying. You'd wonder if any of it was about you.

You'd want to go home.

"I was out with Lily, who I thought I liked a lot, when a few of her friends showed up at the café. The next thing I knew, she was laughing away with them about something they obviously didn't want to tell me about, and I just sat there feeling like an idiot. I was so mad that I actually felt like I didn't like her anymore."

—Marc

Talking about things that other people present don't know anything about without any explanation is like saying, "I don't care that you're here. You don't matter."

Guys have enough trouble understanding what girls are thinking and vice versa. Add secretive conversations and unexplained giggling to the mix, and the boy could just decide to quit before things get really ugly.

So the next time someone tries to start a private conversation with you when you and your date are out with a group of friends, just say, "Let's talk about that later when it's just the two of us."

Your guy will definitely appreciate it. Because—make no mistake about it—every time you disappear into a circle of giggling friends, you're walking away from him.

And if you keep treating him this way, he might end up walking away from *you* one day!

DON'T LET YOUR
DATE GIVE YOU
GRIEF ABOUT
YOUR CURFEW.
THEY'RE YOUR
RULES, NOT HIS.

RAY IS THE COOLEST GUY EVER. ONLY problem is, he's almost two years older than you, and he's not used to 11:30 P.M. curfews. Now you're at a party, and you remind him it's time to leave. He turns to you and says, "Hey, you're not a baby anymore. Can't you hang out until midnight at least?"

You want to say, "Yes! Of course I can!" but unfortunately, you know you can't—your parents would kill you. Instead you stand there, feeling like a five-year-old who's just been scolded for doing something she didn't know was wrong.

It's important to understand that your curfew is not a definition of who you are. It's one of your parents' rules—one they enforce because of their concern for you. Whether your curfew is too early or just right, it's a reflection of *their* thinking and not yours. It's a measure of their particular style of parenting, not whether or not you're mature enough to stay out after midnight.

If anything, abiding by your parents' rules is a sign that you're mature enough to have a mutually respectful relationship with your parents.

You don't need to feel bad or apologize to your date, especially if he knew the rules beforehand. You can say, "I wish we could stay out longer, too. I'm sorry." But you should also make it clear that you're not going to ignore your parents' rules and get into trouble just because your date is used to hanging out later. So try saying something like, "I don't like that my parents want me home so early, but coming in late will only make things worse. They won't trust me anymore, and I won't be able to go out at all." Or, "I wish we could hang out longer, but my parents are strict. Believe me, I'm working on it."

"I was so embarrassed that I had a curfew, I didn't tell Jim until it was time to leave the party. It was 11 P.M. Big mistake. I think he was actually more annoyed that I hadn't told him up

front about my curfew than because we had to leave. He kept saying, " 'How come you didn't tell me?' "

—Megan

When you're honest and don't act embarrassed or make up silly excuses like, "I just remembered I forgot to feed my goldfish!" or break into a childish temper tantrum—"I hate my parents!"—your date will probably be more sympathetic and less critical. He might even have some respect for how you're handling the situation. You're obviously not happy, but you understand that following the rules is your best chance of getting your parents to relax them.

If he continues to berate you for having to leave early, recognize it's his problem. His need to angrily insist on independence is not a mark of his maturity. It's a sign that he may be quite childish in his inability to incorporate the needs and concerns of others into his own life, which could lead to future problems in your relationship.

IF HE ALWAYS
ASKS YOU OUT AT
THE LAST MINUTE,
TELL HIM TO
THINK AGAIN.

YOU REALLY LIKE ALEC, AND YOU'VE been spending a lot of time with him, both alone and with other friends. You're not exactly a thing yet, but it feels like it's getting there. The problem is, he always asks you to do something at the last minute.

You keep saying yes, sometimes canceling your other plans, because you like him. But somehow it doesn't seem right. You're starting to feel like an afterthought instead of someone he really respects and makes time to see. You're starting to wonder if you should be taking his invites seriously. Maybe you're just a convenience date. Still, it sure didn't seem that way the other night when you were making out. . . .

His behavior is making you feel unimportant. However, at this point you don't really have enough information to know what his actions mean. Maybe he really cares but isn't thinking. Or maybe he doesn't care all that much and is only hanging with you to keep busy. Once you know the answer, you'll know what to do.

You have two choices. First, you can lay out the problem directly. Next time he asks you to do something with moments to spare, say, "Alec, I'm not sure why you always ask me to do things at the last minute, but it makes me feel like seeing me isn't so important to you. After all, I could have plans. . . ."

If he says, "Oh, I'm really sorry. I don't mean to make you feel bad. I kind of expect to see you, I guess. I probably shouldn't, though. Next time I'll ask sooner," you'll have your answer and feel better. You found out how he feels about you, and you've let him know you don't like being taken for granted.

If he says, "Well, I kinda don't like to make plans that far ahead. I never know what's going on . . . ," you've got another situation. He may be more interested in finding out what other cool stuff is happening than he is in reserving time for you. In this case, you can say, "Well, okay. But just so you know, I like to make plans in advance." Then wait and see what happens. If he continues to call at the last

minute, the relationship probably isn't that important to him. If he does make an effort to call you
earlier to make plans, you'll know he's genuinely
interested in you but was embarrassed to admit he'd
been handling it without thinking.

Your second option is to say nothing directly,
but the next time he asks you to do something at
the last minute, say, "Oh, too bad, I would have
loved to, but I made plans with a friend two days
ago to go to the movies. . . ." (Not just, "Sorry, I'm
busy," which won't clue him in to anything.) This
way you'll be letting him know what he has to do
in order to spend time with you, making it clear
that you can't see him on a moment's notice
because you're the type of girl who likes to make
plans in advance. Try this once or twice, and if he's
really interested, he'll start calling you in advance.
If he doesn't change his last minute habits, you
can probably assume that while spending time with
you is nice, it's just not all that important to him.

Better to know that sooner rather than later so
you really *can* make plans . . . with someone who
cares!

IF YOU AND YOUR BEST FRIEND LIKE THE SAME GUY, TALK IT OUT.

BETWEEN YOUR SOCCER PRACTICES and your best friend's baby-sitting jobs, it seems like it's been weeks since you've had the chance to get together and really talk. But now you've got the whole night to gab away. You can't wait! Especially because you're dying to tell Kaitlin about your big news. You've got a new crush!

"Kaitlin," you begin as soon as the two of you are alone in your bedroom. "I'm in love!"

Kaitlin giggles. "Me too!" she says, grabbing your arm. "How cool is that? Who is it?"

You close your eyes, picturing your crush's adorable brown eyes. "Joe Brander," you say.

The room is silent. You open your eyes.

Kaitlin is staring at you with a horrified expression on her face.

> "Bu-But," she stammers. "That's who I like, too."

It happens. A lot. But before you start attacking each other with the sharpest hair accessories you can find, take a deep breath. First, what the two of you need to keep in mind at all times is how much you value your friendship. Once you realize how important your friend is to you, you'll know there are two things you can't do. And that is to lie or be unfair. You can't say, "Oh, you can have him," and then flirt with the guy behind your friend's back. You can't say, "Oh, I don't care. You take him," and then resent her when she does. You can't claim, "I said it first!" because realistically, what does that matter? And you can't say, "If you really valued our friendship, you'd let me go for him because you just had a boyfriend last month." It's not like we're talking about who gets the last slice of pizza.

The only thing you can do is discuss the situation. Calmly.

And there are a number of ways to work it out.

- You can decide that no guy is worth ruining the friendship you two have and agree to forget about this guy as a potential boyfriend. This may be easier said than done, but let's face it, there are plenty of other guys around—just make sure you both don't go after the same one again!
- Or you can decide to "let the best woman win." In this case, you each can try to win him over. Ultimately it's up to him, anyway. A risky alternative since you may find yourselves in such a heated competition that you start to resent each other.

"I could not believe it when my friend Pam announced she liked this guy I've had a crush on for months. I told her, 'How could you?! You know I like him!' She looked at me kind of annoyed and said, 'But there's nothing happening between you two. And I've always liked him, too. I just never told you because I knew you'd flip out on me. What do you want me to do?' I couldn't really answer her. I mean, she was right. Nothing was happening between me and this guy. But I guess I felt like if I couldn't have him, I didn't want her to have him, either. " —Kara

- Or you can decide to flip a coin and take turns. If she wins, she can go after him. If you win, you do. The other has to hang back until it's clear whether or not he's interested. If he does seem to like her, then you had better back off. If he seems to like her only as a friend, then you still have a chance. This option could still be rough since one of you might feel some resentment, thinking, Well, if he'd known I was interested, maybe it would have turned out differently.

- Or you can decide that neither one of you will do a thing and you'll just wait and see if he starts to show more interest in one of you. This will be a true test of your friendship—if you're both really into him, it's going to be hard to hide it.

" I kind of liked this one girl named Debbie, but her best friend kept coming over to me and stuff. I didn't want to make her feel bad, but I wanted to be with

Debbie more, so I kept asking her to invite Debbie along. I could tell it made her mad, but I couldn't figure out what to do. I kinda thought Debbie liked me, too, because I caught her staring at me a few times." -Kyle

This isn't an easy dilemma. But you have to try to deal with it as openly and honestly as you can. The most important thing to remember is that no two friends are exactly alike. You're a unique and special individual. So if you and your friend like the same guy and he ends up asking her out, it doesn't mean that she's a winner and you're a loser. It just means that for whatever reason, you're not right for that particular guy and he isn't right for you. Remember, the guy you do end up with will be someone who totally clicks with you and will admire you for all your unique traits. And your girlfriend won't mind a bit—in fact, she'll be thrilled for you!

DON'T EAT
LIKE A BIRD
ON A DATE.

ZOE STARED DOWN AT HER SMALL salad plate and picked up her fork. She wasn't really a big salad eater, and the lettuce in this one looked pretty wilted. Still, she wanted Jordan to know she was careful about her weight and keeping a good figure. He'd be grossed out if she, like, ate a whole burger or something, right?

Across the table Jordan bit into his cheeseburger and then slathered ketchup all over his jumbo fries. Zoe's stomach started to grumble. She ate another piece of wilted lettuce and then put down her fork. Now Jordan would be really impressed. She had hardly eaten a thing. Score one for thin girl!

"That's it?" Jordan demanded, staring at her plate.

Zoe looked up at him. She wasn't completely sure, but Jordan seemed sort of annoyed. . . .

Look at it this way. When someone asks you out to eat, they usually say something like, "Want to have dinner with me?" They don't say, "Want to watch me while I eat?"

There's a reason for this. Eating together, whether it's at your favorite diner or at a friend's house, is supposed to be a shared experience. It can be satisfying both physically, psychologically, and socially. If you're hungry, it feels great to eat a satisfying, mouthwatering meal. If you're feeling down, it can be comforting to have a nice, warm bowl of soup, and if you're feeling great, a gooey hot fudge sundae can totally hit the spot. But eating together is also a great way to get to know someone. It

provides a good opportunity for intimate conversation and helps people feel like something is being shared and appreciated—together.

On the other hand, one person eating while the other person isn't can create a confusing atmosphere. What if you're at the movies and although you might be enjoying the flick, you notice your date is restless and disinterested? Or what if you asked a friend to play tennis with you, and when you hit the ball to the other side of the court, she just stood there, without even trying to hit it back? Talk about frustrating! Watching someone not eat can feel the same way—lonely, weird, and even a little annoying. It can also make the eater feel extremely self-conscious.

> **"**I took this girl out to this pizza place near our school. I ordered two slices, and all she got was a diet Coke. I felt kind of funny, I mean it was lunchtime, and I kept saying, 'You sure you don't want any?' She kept saying no, but she was staring at my pizza like she was starving. It was totally messed up. I couldn't wait to get out of there.**"**   —Zach

As for boys liking girls who watch their weight . . . Get real.

Some boys may like girls with slim figures, but every boy has different tastes, and none are terribly interested in how you manage to look as good as you do. Unless you were fifty pounds over-weight and single-handedly shoving a whole seven-layer cake down your throat, it's rare that any guy would think, Man, she needs to watch what she's eating.

So if you're worried about your weight, order something low in calories and eat it. You don't have to pick up your plate and lick it clean, but show your date you're enjoying both the food and the company. Chances are you'll have a better time if you're not worried about your stomach growling so loud your date hears it!

★ RULE # 11 ★

DON'T FLIRT
IF YOU'RE NOT
REALLY
INTERESTED.

YOU HAVEN'T BEEN FEELING SO great about yourself lately. Last month, out of nowhere, Dennis broke up with you, and now Steve just asked you out. Steve's okay, but let's face it—he's no Dennis. You're pretty positive you could never get serious with him.

Still, Steve is really into you, and it makes you feel good. He smiles at you a lot, and he's always hanging around your locker. You're not exactly discouraging him. In fact, you can tell he thinks you're into him, too. BUT WHAT'S WRONG WITH THAT?

A lot.

It may seem like innocent flirting, but put yourself in his position. You're crushing on this guy big time, and he's acting like the feeling is mutual. You're waiting for him to make the big move and ask you out, but he never does.

How do you feel?

Tricked, deceived, hurt, upset, embarrassed, and angry, to name a few not so nice feelings. And you have every right to feel all those things.

But think about what happened. Did he actually make you any promises? Not exactly. At least not in words, but his actions seemed to speak volumes. He was probably just flirting with you, which led you to believe he felt more strongly than he actually did. Maybe he thinks flirting is fun and didn't really think about how you felt. Maybe he did it to make you feel good about yourself. Maybe he did it to feed his ego.

It's not fair to flirt with someone you're not really interested in. In the end, it will only leave the person you're flirting with feeling confused and hurt.

"I was, like, so in love with this girl in my chem class, and it was great because at first I thought she was into me, too. She was always putting her head on my shoulder and joking around with me during lab. I was all ready to ask her out one day when I found

out she was just flirting with me to make another guy in the class jealous. I felt like such a fool. "

-Dave

If you're out with a guy who you think is more interested in you than you are in him, be friendly, but don't flirt. If he reaches for your hand, you might let him take it, but then release it after a short time. If he puts his arm around you, you might let him leave it there briefly so you don't embarrass him, but then move away. If he tries to kiss you good night on the mouth, move your face so that he ends up kissing your cheek. The idea here is to send out the message: "I like you as a friend, but not as a boyfriend." You don't want to abruptly pull away from him—rejection is hard enough—but you do want to let him know gently that things are never going to go further than the "friends" stage.

Flirting is characterized by the promise of affection and implies that there's an attraction that is not being fully acted on. It's also a voluntary action, which you should take responsibility for. It can be fun to flirt if the feeling is mutual, but if you don't really like a guy, don't act like you do. You won't just be flirting with him.

You'll be hurting him as well.

PLAYING IT COOL
IS A WASTE OF
TIME. IF YOU
LIKE HIM, LET
HIM KNOW IT!

YOU'RE HAVING THE MOST AMAZING time with Justin, but you've heard it's never a good idea to let the guy know how you really feel. After all, you don't want him to think he's got you wrapped around his little finger.

"You're great," Justin says, looking into your eyes. "I really like hanging out with you." Then he grabs your hand.

Uh-oh. You have a feeling he's waiting for you to say something nice like, "You are, too. . . ." You really want to smile and squeeze his hand tightly, but you decide to play it cool.

"Thanks," you say instead, and look away.

A second later Justin lets go of your hand.

Oops. Did you do the wrong thing?

Yes, you did. You hurt Justin's feelings. You were so busy protecting yourself by playing it cool, you forgot that making a person feel good is an important part of dating! Sure, if you come on too strong, you might make him overly confident or even scare him off. But if you hang back too much, he's not going to enjoy being with you.

Who would you want to hang out with: Someone who acts like you're nothing special? Or someone who smiles back at you when you look at him?

What you need to do is figure out a middle ground between drowning him in an ocean of giddy excitement and leaving him stranded on an iceberg. If a guy says, "You're really great," or, "I'm having the best time," telling him, "You're great, too," would be nice but wouldn't swell his ego to the size of Yankee Stadium. But throwing yourself at him and gushing, "I'm so so so so glad you feel that way because I think you are the coolest guy in the whole universe and I wouldn't want to be with anyone else," could send him on a huge ego trip and maybe even scare him off. He thinks you're great. He's not asking you to get married!

❝I asked this girl I liked to go skating on Saturday, and we had a blast—at least I thought we did. We were laughing and talking the whole time, and I was, like, stoked. Afterward I told her how much fun I had, and she didn't say anything. It felt like she just ignored me. What's up with that?**❞**   —Brett

The point is, when a guy says, "I like you," he's putting himself on the line. Maybe he had the guts to tell you how he feels because he senses that you feel the same way. By holding back and playing it cool, you're not only avoiding the truth but making him feel foolish.

And that's really not cool.

✳ RULE # 13 ✳

IF YOU HAVE A
CRUSH ON AN
OLDER GUY,
DON'T TRY TO
GROW UP FAST.

THE MINUTE YOU LAID EYES ON Jeff, you felt like you were going to pass out. He's beyond gorgeous! Only problem is, he's a high school senior and you're only a freshman. Still, everyone says you look a lot older. You don't think he's noticed you yet, but you're not really worried. You're sure he will.

And in the meantime you'll get rid of those immature decorations in your locker and start dressing more sophisticatedly. . . .

The question is: Are you dressing up to create another person? Or getting dressed up to feel good about yourself? Dressing up in something more sophisticated than your usual jeans and T-shirt for a special occasion like a school dance or a wedding is fine. Everyone knows this is a time to get really decked out. But when you dress up to "trick" others into thinking you're someone that you're not, then you're acting a part, and that's no way to begin a relationship.

Chances are the older guy you're crushing on is acting his age. But you might be changing your behavior, pretending to be older than you are. It may even work for a little while, but eventually he'll figure it out, or you'll begin to feel the strain of trying to be someone you're not, or both. The real you can't help but shine through, and it's nothing to be ashamed of!

An older guy is going to need and expect particular things from a girlfriend his age. He may expect her to understand him in ways only a girl facing similar issues—like college—really could. He may want to be with someone who could stay out as late as he can and whose friends he'd feel comfortable hanging out with. Like you, he's still growing and learning—leaving one stage behind and moving on to another. But you're both in different stages of your lives, and he'll ultimately need a girlfriend who can move with him.

For the same reason, you need someone who's in the same place as you are. It might be someone inexperienced with relationships, struggling with his parents' rules, but someone who can hang out with your friends without feeling out of place or without you feeling self-conscious. A boy closer to your age can give you this. A much older boy can't.

“I have kind of a curvy body. More curvy than the kids in my grade. I can make myself look older, which I thought was great because I had a crush on a guy almost three years older than me. He didn't know I was a freshman. He thought I was at least a sophomore. So I put on tight clothes and extra makeup, and we went out and then he started to throw himself on me and I got really scared. I actually asked him to take me home. When I got there, I was so mad, I started chucking half my new makeup into the garbage. The thing is, I'm not sure who I was really mad at. Him or me.”
—Allison

Any girl can make herself look older if she wants to. You can dress sexy, walk in a provocative way, and try to talk like some of the older girls in your school. But that's all superficial. Clothes aren't what makes someone more mature. Only experience does that, and the longer you live, the more experience you'll have.

Besides, what really keeps relationships together is the stuff that comes naturally, from the inside. The thoughts that pop up from nowhere, the clothes you impulsively throw on because they feel like "you," and the natural way you move through your life attracting those who care for your "real" personality. Performances can be entertaining for a while, but they're impossible to keep up. Think of what would happen if an actor in a play could never take a break from a role he was playing—not even when he was just hanging out with his friends. He'd probably feel like he was losing it big time!

So if you have a crush on an older guy, enjoy it from a distance. If you want to, you can fantasize about the guy. Imagine how sophisticated and mature you would feel with him by your side. Think of how grown-up and exciting it would be to go out with him. Maybe you can't have it now, but years down the road, when the two of you have both been through all the major stuff like going to college and leaving home . . .

In the meantime, dress in your own clothes and love yourself for who you are now *and* who you'll become. After all, the real you is the only one worth noticing. So don't hide her!

YOU DON'T
HAVE TO
BUNGEE JUMP TO
IMPRESS A GUY.

"SO CHECK THIS OUT—WE'RE RIDING our bikes down this narrow mountain path," Alex is saying, "and the trail is majorly rocky, and we almost go crashing into this ravine! It was so freaky!"

"Wow," you say, trying to look impressed.

Alex's face lights up. "Hey, want to go back there with me next weekend?" he asks excitedly. "You could borrow my sister's bike!"

Yeah, right, you think. You'd rather watch Barney videos with your bratty little brother—at least that would be safer. Still, this is your second date with Alex, and he's so unbelievably cute. You don't want to blow it. . . .

It's definitely a be-yourself moment.

Easy to say, right? But what if "yourself" is a total bore with a capital *B*?

To begin with, that's the wrong question. The right question is, "What if who I am isn't who he wants?"

Just because you're not into risking your life cycling down rocky mountain roads or piloting a Jet Ski through shark-infested waters or skiing down a double-black-diamond trail doesn't mean you're a bore. It just means you like to be challenged in other ways.

The same thing would apply if you were dating a guy who had you laughing your head off every five minutes when you can barely remember the punch line to a joke. You can't do a stand-up comedy routine if it's not what you have a talent for. This doesn't mean you don't have a sense of humor or aren't creative. You're just different.

"Jason loves golf. He'd been trying to get me to play it with him forever, so finally I agreed to go. While we were on the course, he asked me, 'You don't like this much, do you?' I felt sick. I was sure he was going to break up with

me. 'Um . . . well . . . It's all right, I guess,' I managed to choke out unconvincingly. Jason cracked up. 'Don't sweat it. It's not like I'll only like you if you play golf. I'll just go with the guys next time. It's sort of a drag to play with someone who's not into it, anyway.' For a second I felt terrible. But he just smiled and said, 'Don't worry. It would be boring if we both liked exactly the same things.' I loved him for that. "
—Jessica

When you feel yourself worrying that you're not *enough* for someone else, remind yourself that being "less than" isn't the issue. Instead the question is: Can you learn more about each other through your differences, or will they simply leave you with nothing in common?

Once you ask that question, you won't worry so much about how you measure up to your date. You'll be more concerned with finding ways to share your talents in a way both of you can appreciate. So when he asks if you'd like to ride a bike over steep and dangerous terrain, you'll feel completely confident saying no. But you might suggest riding on paved roads instead, or would that be too boring for him?

Then it'll be his turn to worry. He probably didn't mean to come off sounding like some psycho dare-devil.

After all, who'd want to date someone like that?

Sometimes your interests will be so radically different that even though you and a boy might be seriously attracted to each other, what you each want to do in your time together will be a never-ending source of conflict. In that case, you may just have to give up trying to get along and call it quits.

That doesn't mean either one of you is a bore.

It means you're bored with each other. There's a big difference.

So go ahead, girl—be yourself. It's what makes you *you*!

DON'T BE
AFRAID TO CALL
IT QUITS—EVEN
IF IT MEANS
BEING SINGLE
FOR A WHILE.

> FACE IT. THINGS WITH BEN HAVEN'T been so great lately. His stupid jokes have been getting on your nerves, and he never seems to really get what you're saying. It's like you're speaking two different languages or something. Ben's not as hot as you used to think he was, either. Plus you're starting to boss him around and ignore what he says, which makes you feel like a horrible person.
>
> The trouble is, you can't bring yourself to break up with him.
>
> You hate not having a boyfriend. . . .

Staying in a relationship with someone you don't really like just because you don't want to be alone is never a good idea. You might be thinking, Well, at least I *have* a boyfriend. On the contrary, you're more likely to feel lonely and miserable when you're stuck with the wrong person.

Still, when you picture yourself going to parties alone or spending a Saturday night with your parents watching bad made-for-TV movies, suddenly a boyfriend, *any* boyfriend, sounds like the better option.

That is, until you consider what's really going on.

First of all, you're hurting someone. Chances are if you're not happy, your boyfriend isn't happy, either. How could he be? No one wants to be in a relationship with someone who obviously doesn't care about them. But for whatever reason, he's not willing to make the move and tell you he wants to break up. So he's pretty much become your punching bag.

Second, it's hard to feel good about yourself when you know you're hurting your boyfriend's feelings. After all, this is someone you once cared about, at least a little bit. It's almost like you're *too* in control of the relationship, sort of like one of those bullies everyone hated in elementary school.

And last of all, your friends have probably noticed that you're not the happiest couple in the world, which makes them feel uncomfortable. It's unpleasant to hang out with two people who are always at each other's throats. They might feel pressured to side with you, but what if they think *you're* the one being mean and insensitive? Are they being disloyal by siding with your boyfriend? Do you really want to risk your friendships over a boy you don't even really like?

"My best friend, Morgan, was going out with this guy I knew she didn't really like anymore. She was so mean to him. I couldn't stand to be around them. It was embarrassing. One day I actually told him to break up with her! He was a nice guy, and I figured she'd get over it." —Emma

Finally, there are the missed opportunities. While you're battling it out with Mr. Not Right, feeling lonely, or feeling like the bully you never wanted to become, you may be missing a chance to start something with Mr. Right. You may even be giving Mr. Right the completely wrong impression of the kind of person you really are! You're so hung up on your current unhappy situation that you can't see the world around you clearly or give people a chance to see the real *you*.

Think about it. Being without a boyfriend doesn't necessarily mean you're going to feel lonely. It might simply mean you're "on your own." These are two different states of being and don't necessarily have anything to do with each other. It's easy to feel lonely when you're with someone. And it's possible to feel perfectly fine on your own. In fact, you'll probably have more luck with your next relationship if you're on your own first. You'll feel more independent, confident, and available to meet new people, and all of your energy will be directed outward. Why? Because you finally sawed off that ball and chain—aka the wrong guy!

So if you know in your heart it's time to break up, don't be afraid. Do it. Singledom will *not* be permanent. Just think how free and open you'll be to all the new and exciting possibilities out there. Sticking with a rotten relationship will only drag you down—and everyone else involved will be brought down with you. Bad idea, right?

IF HE SAYS HE
DOESN'T WANT
A SERIOUS
GIRLFRIEND,
BELIEVE HIM.

YOU AND CRAIG HAVE BEEN SEEING each other on and off. It seems like the two of you are getting closer, but there are still lots of times when he's not around and seems to be perfectly happy hanging out with the boys. He's told you he doesn't want a serious girlfriend, but you think maybe things are changing. You had always hoped they would. In fact, you think you might be winning him over.

Last night you found out the truth. The two of you were heading home after a party, and you found yourself blurting out, "Craig, what do you think about us really going out . . . like a real boyfriend-girlfriend thing?"

Craig stopped and looked at you with genuine surprise. "Don't get me wrong," he began. "I really like hanging out with you. But I told you before—I'm not really into having a serious girlfriend or anything."

You know you shouldn't be shocked, but you feel like someone just karate kicked you in the stomach.

Welcome to the time-honored trap titled "I'll Be the One to Change Him." It's a trap we all set for ourselves at one time or another when we really like someone who doesn't want to be tied down by a relationship. We tell ourselves, "Yeah, but with me it's going to be different."

One thing is absolutely, completely certain: No matter how hard you try to change him, it won't work. Only *he* can change him. Don't delude yourself by thinking you have the beauty, the personality, the magic trick that will turn a frog into a prince.

He's told you he doesn't want to get serious, but you've been harboring secret fantasies that the more you hang out together, the more attached to you he'll become. There is a tiny, vague chance that this could happen. But it's unlikely. So you have to take him at his word: He doesn't want a girlfriend.

It's too unfair to *you* to do otherwise. The pressure to be "the one" is just too much to take. You can't be because he's not looking for anyone. And when you don't succeed in turning him around, you'll wind up punishing yourself unnecessarily—obviously something wasn't good enough about you. Wrong. It's kind of like a lawyer presenting a case in a courtroom to a jury that's already made up its mind before it walked in. If none of the members of the jury are willing to give the lawyer a chance, nothing he says, none of his brilliant tactics, will change their minds. Does that make him a terrible lawyer? Of course not.

"I was sure Paul would change his mind. He always seemed to be having such a good time when we were together. I stopped looking at other guys and did things with Paul whenever he asked. I had a special feeling things were going to work out. But they didn't. Paul started seeing another girl, too, and I was furious. I told him how mad I was, and then he got angry with me. 'I told you I didn't want to be serious. I can see other people if I want to,' he snapped at me. What could I say? He had told me that. I guess I just didn't want to hear it." —Lynn

The next time a guy tells you he doesn't want to get serious, believe him and keep your options open. You simply can't lose that way. If you show the guy you like that you're fine with being independent, he may feel braver about trying a relationship since he won't feel pushed into something he's not ready for. Or you might forget all about him when you meet someone else—someone who wants to be in a serious relationship just as much as you do.

IF YOU KNOW
YOUR FRIEND'S
BOYFRIEND IS
CHEATING, LET
HER KNOW . . .
GENTLY.

YOU'RE ALWAYS SEEING THINGS you're not supposed to. Did you have to go to the bookstore last night? There you were, innocently searching for a book, when suddenly you spotted Sam, your best friend Jyl's boyfriend, making out in the corner with a girl you hardly know. They didn't see you, but you definitely saw more than you wanted to.

Just last night on the phone, Jyl was telling you how much she likes Sam and that their relationship is so good. What a joke.

Today you're supposed to meet her at the mall. Should you say anything? Should you tell her what you saw?

Before you go into panic mode, realize that things may not be as bad as they seem. You witnessed a few seconds of something, and while it did look like Sam was cheating, you don't know this for a fact.

- Maybe it was an old girlfriend who suddenly threw her arms around Sam's neck and started kissing him, and he couldn't or wouldn't push her away.
- Maybe the girl came on to Sam, and at that moment he just couldn't resist. But he regrets letting it go that far because he really cares about Jyl.
- Maybe, in a moment of weakness, Sam asked another girl out just to see what it would be like to be with someone else, and even though he kissed that girl, the whole time he was thinking, Man, I wish I was with Jyl!

"I couldn't help myself. I met this girl from another town when I was at a football game with my friends. I could tell she really liked me, and even though I knew I was with Megan, I just had to see what it would be like. So I hooked up with the girl, and I liked her and everything but

I kept thinking about Megan. I felt really guilty. But actually, I liked them both. So I did something stupid and tried to see them both. What a mess. Before it was over, half the girls in school thought I was, like, this big womanizer. " —Andrew

Here are a few things to remember. Your friend and her boyfriend aren't married. They're not even engaged. They're young and still learning about the kind of people they like to be with and how to behave in a relationship. This doesn't mean that they should be disloyal, dishonest, or hurtful to each other. But they're allowed their ups and downs, and they're allowed to work out their confusion in ways that are difficult to understand.

So before you do or say anything, it might be wise to keep quiet and keep an eye out for your friend. Does it appear during the following week that Sam is being caring toward Jyl, or is he acting distant and unavailable and generally making her unhappy? Is he making plans with her or avoiding her completely? Do you notice him flirting with other girls or treating Jyl in a way you think is unkind, even if she doesn't say anything about it to you?

If everything seems okay, you might want to chalk this up to Sam being an unmarried teenager who needs to sort out how he feels about things and may not always do so in the best, most honest way possible.

If things are going badly and Jyl seems completely mystified or, worse, unwilling to admit anything is wrong although you can tell she's miserable, you might want to tell her to beware. But do so gently. Mention what you saw at the bookstore or try hinting at the fact that you think something is wrong. Here are two options:

If she tells you she thinks something might be wrong, but she isn't sure what it is, try something like:
- "Jyl, look, I was in the bookstore a few days ago, and I saw Sam with another girl. I didn't know what it meant, so I didn't tell you right away. But now that you're saying things aren't going well with Sam, maybe something more serious is going on. I would talk to him. But try not to accuse him of cheating and stuff because he might get mad. Just say you heard he was with another girl at the bookstore and you need him to be honest with you."

If she hasn't said anything about it to you but you can tell Sam is making her unhappy, you'll want to tread lightly since she may not be ready to hear about what you saw. Try something like:

- "Jyl, I get the feeling you and Sam are having some problems. Why don't you talk to him and see what's going on? Isn't it better to know if it isn't working out than to just go on like this? Maybe if you two talk, things will improve." If she insists that everything is just fine, you might want to tell her what you saw in the bookstore. It might be the only way to pull her out of her denial.

The bottom line: Don't jump to conclusions. But if the lying continues and you can see a friend is being hurt, it's probably best to step in and let the truth come out.

Your friend may go a little overboard at first. She may yell at you for not speaking up earlier and then call her boyfriend and make wild accusations, ending their relationship abruptly. You can't control that. And although her immediate reaction might make you feel like the worst friend in the world, she'll thank you in the end.

IF YOU SENSE
YOUR CRUSH IS
TOO SHY TO KISS
YOU FIRST, GO
FOR IT!

YOU'RE HAVING SUCH AN AWESOME time with Mark. This is the second time you've been alone with him, and you can't believe how hot he is. You really wish he'd grab your hand, or put his arms around you, or maybe even dive in for a kiss. Nothing really major, but something. But he's just standing there, smiling and staring deep into your eyes. That's it. You're pretty sure you've been sending off the I-want-to-kiss-you vibe for the past hour. What is he waiting for?

There has never been a rule stating that the boy must be the one to initiate a kiss. But it's certainly always been the tradition. Males are supposed to be strong and aggressive, and females are supposed to be weaker and passive. Of course, we all know that's not always the case. Just look at some of your girlfriends—would you call every one of them weak and passive? Sometimes you just have to throw those old stereotypes out the window—especially if every bone in your body is shouting, "I want this, and I don't think he'd mind!"

So before you get bent out of shape because your crush isn't making the first move, remember that he could be scared for the same reasons you are. People can feel very vulnerable when they're attracted to someone. They don't want to be rejected. They don't want to find out the feeling isn't mutual. Maybe they sense that things are going well, but they're too shy to take that next critical step.

"I was with this really beautiful, cool girl, and I wanted to kiss her, but I was afraid she'd laugh at me. I think she liked me, but I just couldn't put myself out on a limb like that, so I chickened out. It was horrible. I heard she started dating someone else a couple of weeks later." —Sam

Maybe you're not shy and you're not afraid to take a chance. What are you going to do? Just stand there and allow old stereotypes to run your life?

Naturally, you don't want to throw yourself at your date, smother him with kisses, and leave him gasping for breath, beet red with embarrassment. Keep in mind that he's shy, and move forward gently, encouraging him to kiss *with* you.

What's the best way to do this? Check out the quick tips below for some hands-on or, in this case, lips-on instruction:

- Put your hands on his shoulders and step close. Tilt your head up to meet his gaze with a soft smile, looking deep into his eyes. Brush your lips gently against his and then pull away.

or

- Put your arms around his neck and say, "I'm going to kiss you now—is that okay?"

or

- Put your arms around his neck and say, "Would you like to kiss me? Because I would really like to kiss you."

"It was really cool. I felt kind of grown-up. I just said, 'Matt, I'm going to kiss you.' I said it with

a giggle, though, and he looked at me, sort of surprised. 'You are?' he asked. And then he moved a little closer. It was like he gave me this green light." —Kristin

Remember, don't leave any room for doubt. A shy boy might need the truth spelled out for him. So be direct and show him how you feel.

Kiss him!

DON'T CONFUSE
FORBIDDEN
LOVE WITH
SOMETHING IT
ISN'T: REAL.

YOU CAN'T STOP THINKING ABOUT
Nathan. When are you going to see
each other next? Will anyone catch
the two of you together? Everyone
thinks that Nathan and Jenna are so
in love, but it isn't true. It's you he
loves. You can't wait for him to tell
Jenna the truth so that you can
finally be a couple. In the meantime
you're supposed to meet him at the
Starbucks on the other side of town.
Just thinking about seeing him
there, secretively waiting, sends a
thrill up and down your spine. This
is definitely it—true love.

Forbidden love always feels intense. Deeply
meaningful. Desperate, even. It can be utterly
intoxicating.

But what's probably fueling this avalanche of
exciting emotions is the fact that you and this boy

shouldn't be together in the first place. The idea that someone will see you together, that you're too attracted to each other to control yourselves despite the danger, that no one understands your passion, creates very high drama. Who wouldn't want to be part of a sexy Hollywood movie? You can even see the trailer now:

FORBIDDEN LOVE THAT COULD NOT BE DENIED
THE QUESTION IS, ONCE ALL THE SNEAKING AROUND IS OVER, WILL YOU STILL LIKE EACH OTHER?

"Derek and I were so hot for each other. But he was going with someone else. He didn't want to tell her yet, so we started sneaking around. We met at the duck pond in a park near my house. We went to the McDonald's in the next town. We even met at my house when my parents weren't home. We were sure we were in love. Then finally he broke up with his girlfriend, and we 'came out.' Only then I started to notice that his sense of humor could get kind of dumb. In about a week I wasn't so sure about us anymore." —Gail

Sometimes when the thrill of someone being off-limits is gone, so is the passion.

Under normal circumstances, the first phase of a romance is spent checking each other out, asking questions like, "Does this person understand me? Do we like to do the same things? Do we laugh together?" This process often gets skipped over in a forbidden relationship, when "How can we be together?" is the most pressing concern. When that's taken care of, the two people involved are suddenly forced to get to know each other under very embarrassing circumstances. *They're already together!*

This is not to say that forbidden love that suddenly gets handed a license can't work. It can. But because the focus of the relationship will no longer be, "What are we going to do—we must be together, and no one will let us!" you need to make a smooth transition into real boyfriend-girlfriend status.

You may not be able to control your passion while one of you is technically off-limits. But remember that once you work out how to be together openly, you still have a lot to learn about each other. Spend quality time getting to know each other and each other's friends and family. If the relationship was meant to be, this won't take away from the romance; it can only strengthen it. Real relationships are far more romantic than forbidden ones.

So, when you and your forbidden love are finally free to be together, first make sure that you're both as keen about being together as you were when you were sneaking around. If you're both into it, start getting to know each other.

Actually, that can be really exciting . . . not to mention *very* real.

DON'T TELL A BOY
THAT YOU DON'T
LIKE HOW HE
KISSES. INSTEAD
TRY A LITTLE
SHOW-AND-TELL.

YOU AND CRAIG ARE MAKING OUT for the second time, and it's no better than the first time. He's kind of a sloppy, wet kisser. He probably thinks he's being passionate and romantic, but you're getting kind of grossed out. It's like you're making out with a Saint Bernard!

You like Craig, but how can you tell him he needs to sign up for some serious kissing classes?

Well, you just can't say, "Listen, you're a really gross kisser." He'll be out the door before you open your eyes! You can't even say gently, "I don't like it when you kiss me that way." No matter how nicely you try to say it, he'll be insulted.

What you can do is show him what you like by doing it, and maybe talk him through it. Kind of like a kissing coach.

If he's being too aggressive, pull away a little bit and kiss him softly on the mouth once or twice. If he doesn't catch on and lighten up on his kissing technique, then try adding a few comments like, "This is nice . . . ," you might say as you kiss him lightly. "I like to kiss softly, too. . . ." That way you've almost made it seem like the change in kissing style is partly his idea!

If he goes back to the kind of kisses you don't like, pull your mouth away again and say something like, "Sometimes when we're kissing like this, I feel like I can't breathe. Can we try to do it a little softer? Like this . . . ," and kiss him softly.

Chances are he won't feel like you're accusing him of being a bad kisser because you've said, "When *we're* kissing," and not, "When *you* kiss me . . ."

"I was really upset! I liked this guy a lot, but the first time we started kissing, it was awful. He kept jamming his tongue in a lot and smashing his face into mine. It just felt bad. So bad that I really didn't want to make out again. At least, not like that. So I asked him, 'Can we kiss another way?' For a second he looked a little upset, but then I started showing him how I liked it, and he got into it. I felt so much better." —Renee

But what if he's not a passionate enough kisser?

Well, you can show him that, too, but not too aggressively! Kiss him a little longer and a little deeper than he's used to. Then pull back with a smile and say, "That felt good. You're such a great kisser." Chances are he'll catch on pretty quickly.

By showing him what you like instead of accusing him of doing what you don't like, you're protecting his feelings and turning it into a much cooler kissing experience.

So have fun, and keep kissing!

RULE # 21

IF YOU KNOW
HE'S ALREADY
TAKEN, LEAVE
HIM ALONE.

> **EVERYONE IN SCHOOL KNOWS JACKIE**
> and Luke are a couple. But Luke is so
> incredible—you have a massive
> crush on him. Jackie isn't really a
> good friend of yours, so you're
> thinking that if you flirt with Luke a
> little bit, you can figure out if you
> have a chance with him or not. After
> all, what have you got to lose?

More than you think.

First of all, when you flirt with another girl's
boyfriend, especially a girl who is in your school
and maybe friends with some of your friends,
you're wearing a sign. The sign says, I Go After
What I Want No Matter What.

You might think your good friends know that
you would *never* try to steal *their* boyfriends. But
that's not the point. It doesn't matter whether the
girl is your best friend or not. Her boyfriend isn't
fair game until they break up.

Going after someone else's boyfriend is like saying

you don't value other people's feelings and boyfriends count more than friends. Your good friends would hope you wouldn't do the same to them, but they would stop trusting you as much as they did before.

Second, what about this couple? Relationships are scary enough. Anyone can get hurt. Do you really want to be responsible for breaking them up?

> **"I** knew things hadn't been going really well with Sam and me, but I couldn't believe it when Claudia started flirting with him. I mean, I was trying to work things out with him. Claudia didn't know this, of course, because we weren't good friends, but still . . . I wouldn't have tried to steal her boyfriend. Sam ended up breaking up with me to go out with her. I don't think they lasted more than a week together. The whole thing was so uncool.**"** —Amanda

What if you do get him in the end? Not too many people are going to be happy for you. Your friends might avoid hanging out with you and him for fear of hurting his ex-girlfriend. They'll have to choose sides.

And what if you don't get him? You'll be embarrassed. You may have lost a few friends, and you'll have nothing to show for it but a bad rep.

So stay away from other girls' boyfriends. If they aren't meant for each other, they'll break up. *Then* you can have a chance with him. By playing it straight, you'll feel good about yourself and better about him. Why would you want a guy with a wandering eye, anyway? If you were able to steal him with a little flirting, maybe he's not very good at being a boyfriend. He might leave you just as easily.

Or he might be the boyfriend of your dreams— someone you'll grow to really cherish. You may even stay together a long, long time. And relationships like that are worth waiting for.

✳ RULE # 22 ✳

NEVER CANCEL
PLANS WITH YOUR
GIRLFRIEND FOR
A BOYFRIEND
(UNLESS IT'S AN
EMERGENCY!).

YOU AND KARA HAVE BEEN PLANNING to hang out together Saturday night for a home spa thing—mud masks, pedicures, hot oil treatments—the works. But Wednesday after school Kevin calls. You've been waiting for him to notice you forever, and now he wants to take you to a party on Saturday night. You're so excited, you can hardly stand it. Except that you don't want to hurt Kara's feelings . . .

You've heard this one many times: *Never break a date with a girl for a boy*. One day you're going to need that girlfriend, and if you don't treat her well now, she may not be there when you need her later. You can't treat people like second best and expect to maintain a lasting friendship. No one likes to be replaced. If you make them feel like they have been, they'll wind up resenting you for it.

As for the boy who got you into this situation—have a little faith! Whatever inspired him to ask you out once will inspire him a second time. He might even become more determined because you kept him waiting—there's nothing like wanting something that's unavailable!

The key is to turn him down the right way so that he knows to ask you out again. Something like, "I'd love to go, but I've already got other plans. Can we do it another time?" This is direct, warm, and slightly mysterious. He may wonder what you're doing (Uh-oh. She has another date!), but he'll also know you want to see him again. If you sense that this guy is kind of insecure, you might want to explain the situation even further. "I'm so sorry, but I already have plans with Kara. Can we get together another time?" That way he'll know you're not turning him down for another guy, which might have made him too nervous to ask you again.

Now, what about those emergencies?

Let's say the boy you've had a crush on for months suddenly asks you to his prom. It's a once-in-a-lifetime situation—let's face it!

The first thing to do is to let your girlfriend know how important she is to you. You'll need to consider how important your date with her is. Were you getting together specifically because she's lonely or depressed? Is she having significant problems at home or trying to get over a bad breakup? If your friend really needs you right now, it would be best to say no to your crush, even if it is the prom.

But if your date with your girlfriend was just regular hang-out time, you can safely postpone it as long as you explain yourself completely: "You won't believe this, but Kevin called and asked me to the prom on Saturday night! You know I would never normally do this to you, but would you be mad at me if we got together next Saturday night instead?" Then try to gauge your friend's reaction.

"My friend called and said she didn't want to make me feel bad, but this guy Tommy that she's, like, in love with got first-row tickets to see this band my friend likes. She knew we had plans, but she was dying to go to the concert. She kept saying, 'I swear I'll never do this again. I just have to go!' I actually didn't mind. It was so obvious that she didn't want to upset me that it was almost funny. I told her it was okay but that one day I'd break a date with her and she'd better be as nice as I am!"

If your friend is okay with everything, think of something cool to do to make it up to her, and then set another date to get together. Schedule the date right then and there so she doesn't feel like you're ditching her cold.

Then go and have a good time with your crush. But be sure you make good on your next date with your friend . . . and the next . . . and the next. Emergencies are rare. If they seem to start cropping up, chances are you're getting into the bad habit of letting guys rule your life.

And you'll be breaking, not bending, this very important rule.

A KISS DOES
NOT HAVE TO
BE A PRELUDE
TO ANYTHING
ELSE.

YOU'RE OUT FOR THE THIRD TIME with Max, a boy you really like. You're at his friend's house with no parents around. The two of you are kissing, and it feels great. Then his hands start to move lightly over your body, and you tense up. It feels good, but sort of like it's too much, too soon.

You pull away slightly and say, "Max, I'm not ready for this. . . ."

He stares at you. "Oh, come on . . . ," he says, one hand trying to sneak up the back of your shirt.

"No, really," you say, a little firmer now as you try to squirm away.

Max sits up and crosses his arms. "So what are we here for?" he asks, clearly annoyed.

It might feel like anything you say in response will sound stupid.

Saying, "To be alone together so we can get to know each other better," could sound too prim, like something your mom would say.

Saying, "I thought just kissing was nice," could make you feel immature.

Saying, "I don't know—maybe I should go home," could make you feel like you just did something bad when you didn't.

So what do you do?

Stick with how you feel, and don't let him pressure you into anything you're not comfortable with. If it doesn't feel right, then it isn't right. Your feelings matter just as much as his in this situation, and every one of the three options above are fine responses. You don't have to go any further than talking to get to know a person. You might want to try kissing, but if you don't want to take it any further than that, don't. There's nothing immature or wrong about being true to yourself. But the only way to communicate what you feel is by talking.

"I couldn't believe it when Maddy stopped us. I thought things were going so well. I was really excited, and she was really kissing me back, and then all of a sudden nothing. She just said, 'Stop. I don't want to do this.' I felt pathetic. Like she hated the way I kissed or something. So I just stood up and went back to the party." —Lee

You need to understand what he's going through, too. When you tell him to stop, he might feel rejected, hurt, physically frustrated, or embarrassed—probably a combination of all of those. And that's tough to take.

When you say "no more" to a boy, you might want to add, "I think you're really cute, but I'm just not ready for this yet." You might also try, "I think you're great, but I want to take things slowly, okay?" Say these things in a strong but understanding voice. A voice that says, "I care about you, but I mean this."

If he has genuine feelings for you, he'll listen. He might still be frustrated, but the rest of the night could continue in an even more intimate way—not physically, but emotionally, because you'll have shared your feelings.

And that's definitely the right prelude to more than just a kiss.

DON'T ASK A
BOY IF HE
LOVES YOU.

> YOU'RE DYING TO KNOW. YOU AND Dylan have been going out for a month, and you really care about him a lot. In fact, it feels like you might be in love with him!
>
> Now the two of you are hanging out at his house, and you're afraid you're going to burst if you don't find out how he feels about you—right now! He has to love you, too, right? All you have to do is ask. . . .

But it's not a simple question.

Love is a very powerful and exciting word.

When two people are in love, they've made a serious commitment to each other. Love brings with it a special kind of intense devotion and respect for each other. It's a kind of connection that can't be easily broken.

But because love is so serious, the last thing you want is to throw the word around without really meaning it.

Unfortunately, there are lots of people who say, "I love you," hoping to mean it. Somehow they think if they say it, it'll be so, and the relationship will instantly grow.

For instance, someone might say, "I love you," hoping to convince you to get physical with them. At the moment of intense attraction it can seem almost true. At other times the words *I love you* might be used just because it seems like the right thing to say. After all, if your boyfriend or girlfriend wants to hear it, instead of hurting their feelings isn't it easier to say the words?

"Jenna said, 'I love you,' and I just sat there. I was like some jerk statue. She started to cry, and I tried to explain I wasn't exactly sure about love but that I knew I really liked her a lot. She just got up and walked away. A part of me felt bad for her, but then another part of me was kind of annoyed at her for putting me on the spot." —Michael

The word *love* should never be used simply to make someone feel good. Sooner or later they'll feel terrible again once they realize what you're saying isn't really true. Similarly, *love* should never be used to fix a relationship. If there's a problem, just saying the word won't make it go away. And you should never say, "I love you," to gain someone's loyalty or coax them into sex. Never use the words *I love you* as a bribe.

But what if you're dying to find out if the word *love* is even in the picture or at least on the horizon?

Try to be patient.

When you ask your guy if he loves you, you're poking your nose into his personal feelings file, without invitation, to satisfy your own needs. Of course, it's only natural to want to hear the words *I love you* from the one that you care for. But the truth is: *Romance can exist without the word* love.

❝I said I love you because I really wanted to hear him say it. I mean, I really thought I loved James. Plus I knew Greg had said it to my friend Stef, and I couldn't help it; I wanted to hear it, too. So James said he loved me back, but he said it so quietly, I could hardly hear him, and I kind of didn't believe he meant it. It was hard to like him after that. I wish I'd never asked." —Ali

Sure, it might seem like hearing *yes* would make you feel great, but chances are it won't. Saying, "I love you," only feels real when it's volunteered. When it's said at a moment when you can sense the two of you are close. Connecting. Caring deeply.

So if you find yourself tempted to ask if he loves you, try to remember that what you really want to know is how he feels about your relationship. Then ask about that instead. It's fair to want to be more certain about the way he feels *about the two of you as a couple.*

For instance, "I'm not sure why, but I'm feeling a little insecure about us. Are we okay? Is there something you think we should talk about? The other night at the party I got the feeling you wanted to be alone. I was kind of hurt that you didn't tell me what was on your mind. Is anything wrong?"

When you ask a guy if he loves you, he might feel trapped because no matter what he says—*yes, no,* or *maybe*—it could have unwanted results. The word *love* carries with it a kind of promise that neither of you may be ready for. If you ask, "How are we doing?" he'll feel less pressured and more able to express himself.

Never forget that how you feel in the relationship is more important than the particular words you hear. You can listen to someone say, "I love you," all day long, but if you don't feel that it's true, it won't make things any better. On the other hand, you can feel completely cared for and truly loved by someone even if they haven't said the words *I love you* yet.

> **"**I almost said 'I love you,' but I wimped out. I was afraid Paul wouldn't say it back and I'd feel like a real dork. So I just kept kissing him. That was easier.**"**　—Amy

If you want to say, "I love you," do so only if you mean it and you're prepared for any response, including the awkward ones.

The words *I love you* should never be used as a pop quiz.

Remember, what really counts in a loving relationship is how the two of you feel about each other and treat each other when you're together. It's like the old saying: Actions speak louder than words.

WHEN A GUY SAYS HE
WANTS TO SPEND TIME
WITH HIS FRIENDS,
HE ISN'T SAYING HE
DOESN'T WANT TO
SPEND TIME WITH YOU.

YOU CAN'T BELIEVE WHAT JUST happened. It feels like you and Ryan haven't had any real time alone together all week, and you've been looking forward to hanging out with him today. But there's a football game on now, and he wants to watch it with the guys.

"What about us?!" you demand.

Ryan hesitates. "Well, you can come, too . . . ," he says, looking at you with puppy dog eyes. "I guess . . . ," he adds.

Talk about a lame invite! Don't do me any favors! you think.

You can't measure how much a boy likes you by the time he chooses to spend with you alone. The fact is, if he spent every waking minute with you and forgot all about his friends, you might be in for more than you bargained for. Constant togetherness isn't a sign of love. It's a sign of dependence. Your boyfriend might be obsessed with you, not in love with you. He might be distrustful of you, not dying for your company. He might feel totally worthless without you and need *you* to help define who *he* is.

So if your guy wants to hang out with his friends, let him. You like hanging out with just your girlfriends sometimes, don't you? Well, he needs that kind of camaraderie, too. Besides, let's face it—do you need him slapping you on your back and yelling, "What a play!" when the quarterback flies across the goal line?

"I didn't know what to do. I know Patti and I didn't spend much time together this weekend, but my friend's dad offered to take us fishing. I never get to do that. So I said yes, and when I told Patti, she went crazy on me." —Adam

Don't forget that while he's hanging out with his friends, you can hang out with yours.

Some girls make the mistake of giving up their friends when they start getting into a guy. But it's important not to let that happen (see Rule #22).

Always remember that your boyfriend can't be all things to you. Besides, doing things with your friends takes some of the pressure off your romance—you don't have to be together all the time to prove that things are going well. And if things don't work out, you'll have your friends to fall back on. Take the time to nurture your friendships—go on an all-day shopping spree, get your nails done together, rent a movie with your best buds and cry your eyes out. After all, if you dump all of your friends and then break up with your guy, who are you gonna hang with?

There's always the possibility, though, that your boyfriend's desire to be with his friends indicates that he's not as devoted to your relationship as you would like.

"The thing is, I get the feeling that I'm what Brendan does when there isn't anything better to do. He says that's not true, but I don't think he tries real hard to see me." —Melissa

Of course you don't want to be with someone who'd always rather be someplace else. That doesn't exactly make for a solid relationship. Your time is too important to spend it with someone who doesn't want to be with you!

So what should you do?

Try expressing how you feel in a way that won't make him feel that he's doing something wrong or that you're on the attack. For instance:

"Ryan, I know you're into watching the game with the guys, but it makes me feel like you never want to be with me."

Hopefully Ryan will understand where you're coming from and explain that his time with you is important, but his friends are important, too. That's fair.

But if he says, "Look, I care about you, but the truth is I need time on my own. Things are getting way more intense than I wanted between us," then you'll know the truth. It's time for you to chill out or move on.

However, it's more than likely that your boyfriend wants to be with his friends so he can just be a *guy*. And there's nothing wrong with that. When's the last time you had fun gabbing with your boyfriend about the hot new guy in your math class? Probably never. That's what your girlfriends are for.

So don't sit around moping—take advantage of your time away from your boyfriend and hang out with your friends. It may sound corny, but it's true: Guys may come and go, but friends are forever!

DON'T BE AFRAID TO ARGUE.

YOU REALLY HATE THE WAY Andrew makes fun of your serious attitude about school. He's an okay student, but you're at the top of your class, and it's important to you that you stay there.

It's Sunday afternoon, and the two of you are hanging out, watching TV at your house. "As soon as this is over," you say, checking your watch, "I've got to start writing that English essay."

"Oh no, you haven't started that English essay?!" Andrew jokes sarcastically. "That's not due until Thursday. You're such a geek sometimes."

You know he's kidding, but you're afraid to tell him that you resent those sorts of comments. Arguments frighten you. What if the relationship blows up?

Here's the funny thing: *Not* arguing causes relationships to blow up far more often than actual arguments do. Many people don't realize this. They think staying away from differing opinions is the way to keep a comfortable peace.

Except it isn't so comfortable, is it? When you fail to speak your mind, you're attempting to put aside how you really feel. Your true feelings stay bottled up inside you, causing you to grow tense, sometimes unhappy, and very often angry and frustrated. These negative feelings keeping building up while your boyfriend has no idea that you're harboring all this resentment. Then, all of a sudden, one small thing sets you off, and you blow up at him. You may even cause a breakup, which is the very thing you were worried about doing weeks ago, when you didn't speak up about wanting to study instead of watching TV.

So the next time you feel the need to express a feeling or an opinion that you think might cause an argument, remember two things. One, there are many ways to say how you feel without necessarily creating a fight. Two, if you do in fact get into a conflict, remember that most arguments have a beginning, a middle, and an end. You can move past them, and you might wind up even closer afterward!

The object is to state what you're thinking in a way that increases understanding and doesn't feel like an attack. If your boyfriend feels like he has to defend himself, he'll be so busy saying, "I didn't do anything wrong!" that he won't hear a word you say. Here are some pointers:

- Begin by telling him that you want to talk about something that's been bothering you. Don't say something has been making you really angry, or he'll immediately tense up. "We need to talk about something that's been on my mind. Please just listen to me for a minute before you say anything."
- Tell him how you feel. Tell him that you like him for who he is, so you feel he should respect you for who you are. "When you tease me about how much schoolwork I do, it makes me feel like you don't appreciate a big part of who I am. I don't want to hide how I feel from you because I like you a lot and I want to be honest."
- Don't tell him he's being selfish. Be sure to stick to your own personal reactions to his words. That way he won't be able to say, "You're wrong." A person's feelings are never wrong.

"My boyfriend told me that he thought I talk too much when I'm with his friends. I got really upset and told him maybe I shouldn't hang out with them or him anymore. He said that's not what he meant, but I went nuts. He was, like, so matter-of-fact, I felt like an idiot. So I just walked away from him. But later that night he called and said he was sorry for being so blunt. . . . At first I was like, whatever, but then he said he liked me a lot, and I calmed down. I told him I might talk more because they all seem to ignore me. He said he'd try not to do that. It felt great to work through that fight." —Kayla

- Finally, tell him what you do need from him. Maybe you need his support and maybe even a little admiration for how well you do in school. After all, you go to his basketball games and cheer him on!

- Then sit quietly, listen to his reply, and try to make sense of any negative reactions he may have. Remember that he may feel just as uncomfortable with confrontation as you do!

If he acts defensive, saying, "I was only kidding. Can't you take a joke?" smile at him and reply, "I know you were only kidding. I don't think you meant to hurt me, but I had to tell you how it makes me feel. It's not a joke to me."

If he says, "You're making a big deal out of nothing," and looks embarrassed, reply firmly, "It's not a big deal. But it's important to me, and I just wanted to make sure I told you."

If he acts annoyed and says, "Well, I thought we were getting along, but I guess we're not," assure him that you have been getting along, but that getting along sometimes means working through your differences.

What happens next is *not* up to you. If he gets bent out of shape and takes off, it's best to let him go. Chances are he'll be back after he thinks about what you said. And if he doesn't come back, you're better off without him. Two people who don't express their feelings honestly with each other don't belong together.

* RULE # 27 *

IF HE KEEPS
TEASING YOU IN
PUBLIC, TELL HIM
TO STOP IT . . .
IN PRIVATE.

YOU'RE OUT WITH A BUNCH OF friends and your boyfriend, Rick, and for some reason he keeps teasing you about your freckles. You know you're too old to be stressing over a bunch of little spots, but you can't help how you feel. They embarrass you, and Rick knows it. He's always telling you he thinks your freckles are cute, but right now, in front of everyone, he's making you feel like a freckle-faced freak! You wish he would just lay off.

"Rick . . . ," you start to say in an annoyed tone of voice after he makes a crack about it being impossible to count all of your freckles. But you don't get any further.

Everyone is staring, your face is getting hot, and you feel like you're ready to explode!

Take a deep breath.

Chances are, Rick's not trying to hurt your feelings. If you yelled at him in public, it would humiliate him and you would lose the opportunity to explain how you really feel about him teasing you. In other words, you could be destroying a chance to actually *strengthen* your relationship. If you blow up at Rick in front of all your friends, you'll wind up embarrassing *everyone* at the table. You might even put an end to your relationship right then and there.

So, what do you do?

You have two options:

When your friends are busy with their own conversations, ask your boyfriend to take a walk with you. Once you're alone, tell him in a very calm but serious voice that you just can't handle it when he teases you. You know he doesn't mean any harm, but apparently he hasn't realized how much it bothers you.

Your second option is to interrupt him when he's teasing you and say, "Come on. You know, I don't think my freckles are all that funny. Can we *please* change the subject?" You risk making everyone uncomfortable if you play it too straight and serious. So smile and maybe say it with mock distress, covering your face with your hands. Then bring up another topic *yourself*. Later, when you and your boyfriend are alone, you can use option one and explain how much it upsets you when he teases you like that.

"I don't have the skinniest legs in the world. I'm more on the muscular side. I was with Dave and a few friends, and he started teasing me about my "tree trunk" legs. I went crazy. I stormed out of the room and ended up sulking in the kitchen by myself. A few minutes later Dave came looking for me. I was waiting for him to start apologizing, but instead he just looked at me and said, "Well, that was really nice." Then he walked out. We haven't spoken since. . . . I guess we didn't have much of a relationship, but I have to admit, I wish we hadn't broken up that way.**"** —Alesha

The bottom line is that there is nothing to gain from causing a scene. You'll embarrass everyone (including yourself), and your boyfriend might be so annoyed that he won't be able to hear or understand your feelings—which is the exact opposite of what you want.

If you want your boyfriend to *really* know you, you have to give him the chance. You may find out that he can't or won't grasp how you feel, in which case you'd be better off without him. But if you express how you feel, and he listens and respects your feelings, you'll be on your way to a strong and lasting relationship.

EVEN IF HE
ONLY SHOVED
YOU A LITTLE
BIT, UNDERSTAND
IT'S ABUSE.

YOUR BOYFRIEND, JEFF, COMES from a pretty messed-up family. His father disappeared a while ago, and his mother works very hard and isn't around much. Jeff has kind of a bad temper and is very possessive of you. The other day he saw you talking and laughing with another guy, and after school he asked you what that was all about. You said that you and Greg are just friends. Which is true.

"I don't believe you," Jeff said in an extremely angry voice.

"But it's true, Jeff," you insist, touching his arm gently.

Suddenly Jeff puts both hands on your shoulders and shoves you backward. "You're lying!" he hisses.

The most important thing to pay attention to here is his use of physical force. It's not the accusations.

It's not whether or not you're lying. And it's not whether or not you can calm Jeff down. It's that he's used his hands in an angry way, on your person, to express his fury.

This is not allowed.

But it was just a little shove, you might argue. Besides, Jeff has so many personal problems. But understand this: No shove is little, and personal problems do not give a person license to abuse other people.

To begin with, small shoves, or light slaps, or tightly gripped wrists, or any physical signs of anger often escalate into bigger acts of violence. Maybe not at that moment, but often as time goes by, a little shove becomes a bigger push, a little slap a bigger punch, and a tightly gripped wrist can become a broken arm. These behaviors are the sign of a person who hasn't learned to control his impulses and use words to sort through problems instead of pushing and shoving. All relationships require two people who can communicate.

"Bruce and I had been going out for two months when it happened. We were meeting at the mall one night to hang out, and I got there late. For some reason, Bruce was convinced that I was trying to break it off with him. He started screaming at me, and then he squeezed my arm so hard, I got bruised. I knew Bruce was upset because of his parents' divorce, and maybe he was just scared of losing me, too. Still, the whole thing really scared me." —Amaya

If he seems unhappy, urge your boyfriend to *talk* about what's bothering him with a trained professional. Be warm, affectionate, and understanding. But don't be his punching bag. He has no right to take his frustrations out on you. And you owe it to yourself to be very clear about the difference.

The next time you feel physically threatened by your boyfriend, speak up: "I will not discuss anything with you if you shove me. You're scaring me. Please stop."

If he doesn't stop or instead of physically hurting you, he begins to verbally insult you, *leave immediately*. Emotional abuse is no more acceptable than physical abuse. It too can be immensely hurtful, and it can escalate into physical abuse.

Remember, no matter what you're arguing about, if he lays a hand on you, *that* is what matters. No matter how small it may seem, it's not right.

DON'T EVER TELL
YOUR BOYFRIEND,
"WHY CAN'T
YOU BE MORE
LIKE . . ."

ANGELA'S BOYFRIEND ALWAYS buys her cute stuff. A sweet postcard, a funny fake ring from a gumball machine, or sometimes even flowers. He's such a sweetie. You wouldn't actually want to go out with him yourself because he's sort of boring. But still. Brad, your boyfriend, doesn't ever give you anything. It's so unromantic.

Maybe you should tell him about Angela's boyfriend—why can't Brad be more like him?

No matter how much you want to tell your boyfriend that you wish he were like someone else, don't say a word! Okay, so he doesn't buy you little gifts. Maybe he's not so patient when you lose the ball on the miniature golf course. Or yes, sometimes he may refuse to dance because he's self-conscious, even though you're dying to get out there and shake your stuff.

But before you open your mouth, take a long, hard look at what you're envying.

Emma's boyfriend may write her little love notes, but is he a good listener?

Sylvie's boyfriend might feel comfortable kissing her in front of everyone, which you think is pretty cool. But is he understanding about the fact that she has to work every Friday night?

And then there's Amanda. Her boyfriend has so much patience teaching her how to snowboard, but what about those rumors that he's sneaking around behind her back?

No one is perfect. If you care about your boyfriend, trust yourself. There must be plenty of great reasons why you like him. Remind yourself of what they are.

Maybe when you talk, he always listens. Maybe he's always willing to help you study for a test. Maybe he's a great kisser and compliments you a lot.

This is not to say that you should accept things you don't like without a peep. But you need to talk about them . . . not shove his inadequacies in his face.

You can say, "It makes me kind of nervous when you laugh at me when we play miniature golf. Give me a break!" Or you can try, "I know it sounds silly, but I would really love it if you gave me a card on Valentine's Day." You can even ask him to dance with you, saying, "I love the way you dance. Please, just one song?"

What you shouldn't say is, "Why can't you be more like Angela's boyfriend? He always buys her stuff." Or, "Jeff never laughs at Amanda." Or, "Look at Matt. He always dances."

First of all, you'll be asking for the following answer. "Okay, so go out with Matt." While this retort might not be very nice and totally ignores the issue, you can hardly blame him. No one likes being compared unfavorably to someone else.

But second and most important, you simply can't change a person. We are who we are. We can learn to be more considerate or sensitive or patient, but we can't adopt someone else's traits. Caring about someone means loving them for who they are, flaws and all.

"I'm not that big on romantic scenes. They make me feel kind of dorky. Like I'm acting in a cheesy movie or something. But my girlfriend wanted candles and everything, so I lit one. Then she wanted me to tell her how I felt about her, and all of a sudden I felt like I really was in a movie, only I didn't want to be. So I told her. She got all pissy and said that her last boyfriend was really romantic. So I told her to go back to him." —Ben

Remember, there are two of you in this relationship. What about you?

You may not be an easy conversationalist. You may be funny, and warm, and interesting, but only in certain circumstances. Wouldn't you feel hurt if your boyfriend pointed out that Jenny can talk to anyone at any time and you can't? Of course you would. You'd rather he told you how honored and special he feels when you open up to him.

Your boyfriend deserves the same treatment. So the next time you wish he were more romantic, or funny, or open, or sensitive, don't compare him to other boys. Talk to him about it. That way you'll stand a better chance of getting all the good qualities of Jeff or Matt or Rob all in one boy—your boyfriend!

* RULE # 30 *

NEVER HIDE ONE
BOYFRIEND FROM
ANOTHER. YOU'LL
END UP WITHOUT
ANY BOYFRIEND
AT ALL.

YOU MET A REALLY COOL GUY AT camp. He lives in another state, and since you got home, you talk on the phone once a week and write each other regularly. You even have plans to see each other soon.

That could be a bit tricky because you've also started seeing this new guy at school. You haven't really talked that much about your relationship yet, but it's pretty obvious neither of you is hanging out with anyone else. He has no idea about your boyfriend from camp, and the boyfriend at camp has no idea you're seeing someone else.

You really like them both and you don't want to choose one over the other. . . . But what will you do when the camp boyfriend comes to visit?

At first glance, it sounds like the main problem is logistics. How, when, and where can you see one boy without the other boy knowing? And while it's understandable and perfectly normal to want to keep both guys in your life, you really need to concern yourself with something else, too.

Them.

Clearly both boys like you a lot and you them. But you're the only one who knows what's going on. And what's going on is that you're keeping from each boy something they ought to know. You aren't exclusively involved with either one of them.

The question is, what do you tell them? How can you be honest without losing either one? This might be beyond your control, but you can try a few careful approaches:

- Call your boyfriend from camp and tell him how much you're looking forward to seeing him. You might add that since the two of you never promised not to see other people, you've been going out with someone at school, and you may want to be careful about running into him when you two are together. Then repeat you're excited about seeing him.
- Call your boyfriend at home and tell him that you really love spending time with him. But the

fact is, before you met, you were seeing a guy at camp who you're still in touch with. He's coming to visit, and you want him to know.

Your boyfriend from camp may feel a little anxious but will probably still want to see you. If you agreed you might date other people when you got home from camp, then all you've done is kept the details to yourself, and he has no reason to accuse you of sneaking around. Of course, if he's been pining away for you, he might feel very hurt, but that's all the more reason to be honest with him.

Your boyfriend from home might be more upset and ask lots of difficult questions like, "Do you like him more than me?" "Do you think about him when we're together?" "Does this mean I can go out with other girls?" In fact, your camp boyfriend may ask some of the same questions.

"Barry and I were kind of boyfriend and girlfriend in camp. We decided we'd talk on the phone after we got home. We ended up talking about once a week. But then I met Roger, and we started to get involved. I didn't mention Barry because he wasn't around. But one time Barry called when Roger was over, and I said I couldn't talk right then. Roger got real uptight when he heard me whispering, so I told him the truth. He got mad at me for not telling him about Barry and almost walked out. So I promised him I wouldn't talk to Barry anymore, but I didn't really mean it. I felt terrible for lying. I started sounding weird on the phone with Barry, and he stopped calling. Then it was just Roger and me, which was okay . . . but I'm still not sure it's what I really wanted. **"**

—Kara

You might feel stuck because you may not know the answers to all the boys' questions. In fact, it's probably a good idea to have some answers on hand before you make any calls. "It's not a question of who I like better," you might tell your boyfriend from home. "It's that he was in my life already. I'm sorry I didn't mention him earlier."

You might want to add, "I wasn't sure if you and I were that serious yet. I'm glad I told you about him, though—I want to be honest with you." To the camp boyfriend you might say, "You don't live nearby, and so I found myself going out with someone. I'm not clear where it's going, and right now I like both of you. I haven't asked if you're seeing someone because I guess I don't blame you if you are. . . ."

And then you'll just have to take what comes. The worst option is to lie to someone you care about. The best way is to lay out the truth and hope they understand. Then they can make their own choices, and you can go forward with a clear conscience and without having to sneak around.

AFTER YOU BREAK
UP, DON'T DIVE
INTO A SERIOUS
RELATIONSHIP WITH
THE NEXT GUY WHO
COMES ALONG.

YOU AND ADAM HAD BEEN GOING out for five months when suddenly he breaks up with you. Actually, now that you think about it, you sort of saw it coming. But even so, you feel terrible. It would be great if the feeling would go away fast.

Then Rich asks you out. Rich is okay. In fact, he's very nice. Sure, you used to think he was sort of dull, but maybe you were wrong. Rich is sweet, and what better way to get over Adam than to start going out with Rich?

Actually, there's a much better way.

Feel bad about the breakup. Give your feelings room, even though it may be painful because they're the truth. Your feelings for the very next guy probably aren't the truth. They're more likely an escape from the pain you're feeling about your breakup. You have to deal with the pain first before you can move on.

Breakups stink. They hurt. They can make you feel insecure and unloved and stupid. They can leave you with the feeling that you'll never be happy again. But guess what? That's normal.

"I was so hurt when Brian broke up with me. I turned right around and started dating Rob, who had always liked me. He was SO happy. And so was I. But after about a week I started feeling kind of crazy. Like I didn't know how I felt about anyone or anything. One night when I was sleeping over at my friend Alana's house, I suddenly started crying about Brian out of nowhere. It actually felt pretty good. Then I ended things with Rob. I think he felt as bad about losing me as I did about losing Brian.**"** –Francesca

Breakups do pass. They lose their sting. They

drop their importance. They become what happened *then*. But only if you allow yourself to feel the pain. If you don't, you'll get involved with inappropriate guys, find yourself in the middle of more messy breakups, and get stuck in a never-ending cycle of quick, unsatisfying romances. Either you'll hurt a lot of guys along the way, or they'll hurt you. If you're stuck on the idea that you have to be with *someone* even if it's the wrong someone, things are bound to get ugly.

So after a breakup give yourself a little time to cry if you need it. Hang out with your girlfriends. Take long, hot baths. Then, when you're feeling strong and confident, you can start going out. Try accepting a date here and there. But don't leap into boyfriend-girlfriend status. You need time to see if someone is right for you. Your head and heart might still be so filled with difficult feelings from your breakup that you won't be the best judge to choose your next boyfriend, anyway.

"I decided about a month ago that I was tired of having relationships that fall apart. It hurt too much. I vowed I wouldn't date anymore. But it didn't stick because I realized it wasn't fun hiding out by myself. I felt kinda dead to the world. So now I go out to parties and stuff, but I'm not looking to get into anything heavy with the next guy I meet. I mean, I think it's better in the long run to take it slow. I'd like to be friends with a guy for a while before I decide if I want him as a boyfriend. For now, I feel like I'm having fun, but I'm not putting any pressure on myself to find someone." —Kim

Don't mistake the next guy who's interested as *the one*. Go slow. Let each relationship teach you something important about yourself and what you want. You'll know when you find a guy too good to let go. In the meantime, relax and have fun so that your head will be clear and your heart will be ready.